Wisdom for Victory

Fruitfulness

Eva Tano-Yeboah

Jesus Joy Publishing

First Published and printed in Great Britain in 2021 by Jesus Joy Publishing.

© Eva Tano-Yeboah, 2021

All rights reserved. The author gives permission for brief extracts from this book to be used in other publications provided that the following citation is stated: 'Wisdom for Victory - Fruitfulness by Eva Tano-Yeboah, 2021; Jesus Joy Publishing used by permission'.

Scripture Quotations

Unless otherwise noted scriptures are taken from THE HOLY BIBLE, NEW INTERNATIONAL VERSION®, NIV® Copyright © 1973, 1978, 1984, 2011 by Biblica, Inc.™ Used by permission. All rights reserved worldwide.

Scriptures noted TMB are taken from The Message Bible New Testament. Copyright by Eugene H Peterson 1993, 1994, 1995. Used by permission of NavPress Publishing Group

Scriptures noted BSB are taken from The Holy Bible, Berean Study Bible, Copyright 2016, 2018 by Bible Hub Used by permission. All Rights Reserved Worldwide.

Cover Design

Cover design by Sabina Baaba Berko

ISBN 978-1-90797-168-6

Jesus Joy Publishing

a division of Eklegein Ltd

www.jesusjoypublishing.co.uk

3105921

Dedication

I dedicate this devotional to the Holy Spirit who in His power and gentleness directs us and transforms us - not giving up, 'till we become like Him.

But the fruit of the Spirit is love, joy, peace, forbearance, kindness, goodness, faithfulness, gentleness and self-control. Against such things there is no law. Those who belong to Christ Jesus have crucified the flesh with its passions and desires.
Galatians 5:22-24

Day 1

Patience

"Bear in mind that our Lord's patience means salvation"

2 Peter 3:15

Patience is defined as the capacity to accept or tolerate delay, problems, or suffering without becoming annoyed or anxious. (Oxford Lexico Dictionary - lexico.com)

Patience is a capacity. It does not come naturally. I remember when we had our first son; as a baby he would scream and shout for his food. No one is born with patience, otherwise babies would know that they do not have to cry for food. I've yet to see a fully grown man scream, shout and burst into tears because food is late. This is because as we mature, we develop more patience, we increase our capacity to withstand problems, go through sufferings and tolerate delay without being anxious, without letting the negative situation define us. Maturity enables us to have a bigger capacity for patience.

Godly patience works salvation and brings out the best in every situation. It will bring out the best in you as a person and the best in the situation in which you find yourself. Once you improve as a person, it will produce a chain reaction of a change in your attitude which will then cause you to have a better perspective of the situation.

Be patient with yourself and allow God to work in you and through you. He works in us initially because we cannot give what we do not have abundantly and overflowing in our own hearts. Whatever God can do through you must most importantly be overflowing in you. When God's work in that particular area of our lives is completed, He can then work through us.

Patience is a sign of maturity. Having an end in mind and keeping your focus on that end no matter the re-routing, is a virtue. Patience is a by-product of a Christ-controlled life.

> *"... imitate those who through faith and patience inherit what has been promised."*
>
> *Hebrews 6:12*

Every promise in God for us will be inherited. If we keep our focus on the promise and not give up or give in; or rush it or lose our peace; or blame God for being unfair. However, if we will go through the problems, the sufferings, the delay and the uncertainties, we will receive every promise far more and beyond what we ever expected because God is faithful.

> *"Now to Him who is able to do immeasurably more than all we ask or imagine, according to His power that is at work within us..."*
>
> *Ephesians 3:20-21*

Reflection

Are you believing God for something that you have not yet received? Is there an area in your life that you wish was more perfect? Are there any terrains where you're not yet victorious? Ask the Holy Spirit to give you grace to be patient in your journey and to pick up every nugget needed to help you come out refined and shining brightly.

Further Reading:

Hebrews 6.

Day 2

Patience

"After Noah was 500 years old, he became the father of Shem, Ham and Japheth... Noah was six hundred years old when the floodwaters came on the earth."

Genesis 5:32, 7:6

We can't focus on fruitfulness without taking a good look at patience, longsuffering or forbearance. They go hand in hand. Patience proves faith and is the force behind bearing fruit. Miracles may happen overnight but patience does not, faith is powered by patience.

In Genesis 5:29 to the end of chapter 7 we see a story of God's patience. God commanded Noah to build an ark to save those who would believe in him. For one hundred and twenty years, Noah built the ark and warned the people of God's impending wrath. For 120 years!

Every single day, God gave these people an opportunity to repent - a chance to turn from their evil ways. Noah through faith in God's word patiently endured the ridicule. Remember it had never rained on earth so the people didn't have a clue what rain looked like let alone understand its potential to destroy the earth. Neither did Noah but he was patient. He went through each day believing God for the salvation his people.

No person is beyond the saving power of Christ and no situation is beyond the resurrection power of the Holy Spirit. Exercise patience. That spouse will change, that child will change, that situation will turn around. You have not yet been on the same issue for 120 years so keep going on. The Lord will turn every situation around for your good. That brother or sister will turn around for the better.

Be patient. Don't be discouraged, don't be overwhelmed, God is working behind the scenes, keep trusting and keep believing.

As a wife, I've also needed to work on my own patience in believing God to change some things about my husband and waiting on God to do His work without my interference and complaints. Looking back, I've developed better character through patience, and my patience with God has proved to me that I had faith in what I was asking for. There were times I prayed, God didn't answer as quickly as I wanted so I gave up on the first prayer and started asking God for something else and then realised that I didn't have faith at all regarding the initial prayer!

Beloved, our patience proves that we have 100% belief in Him who has promised and in what He has promised.

Reflection

> Are you believing God for a change in a spouse, a child or a loved one? Don't stop praying, don't stop believing. Don't let the enemy discourage you. Let your patience nurture your faith that God will answer your prayer. Give God time to work and while He's working praise, worship and adore Him as if it's already done.

Further reading:

> Genesis 6 and 7.

Day 3

Endurance

"Jesus told them another parable: The kingdom of heaven is like a man who sowed good seed in his field. But while everyone was sleeping, his enemy came and sowed weeds among the wheat, and went away. When the wheat sprouted and formed heads, then the weeds also appeared."

Matthew 13:24-26

Jesus used stories to engage his listeners. In this parable, we learn of a farmer who went to sow seed. My mother had a backyard garden that we worked in as kids. And I remember she taught us to sow corn seeds or cassava sticks very early in the morning while the dew was still falling or in the early evening when the sun was setting. She taught us not to sow when the sun was up. So, you can imagine the hard work put in by this farmer to sow on his farm. But the Bible states that when the seeds started germinating, there were weeds with the seed. These particular weeds looked exactly like the wheat that was sown.

The first option was to uproot the weeds but because they were identical with the wheat, there was a high likelihood that the wheat could be uprooted with the tares so the farmer commanded that the tares be left to grow with the wheat until the harvest.

Brethren, this is a great story of patience and endurance. The tares grew side by side with the wheat. They were nourished by the food intended for the wheat. The farmer had to cultivate the tares alongside the wheat all in the hope that he would not lose even one stalk of wheat.

In our struggle against the enemy, let's keep our focus on the good, otherwise we may destroy the good with the evil.

Let us not be hasty to give up on a person, a family, a church, a career or a community. When all things come to fruition, and they do, the Lord of the harvest - our heavenly Father - shall separate the tares from the wheat. He shall pull up the tares first, bundle them, burn them and call us into His glory. Nothing shall be lost, no one shall fall by the side.

> *"Then those who feared the Lord talked with each other, and the Lord listened and heard. A scroll of remembrance was written in his presence concerning those who feared the Lord and honoured his name."*
>
> *Malachi 3:16*

There is a scroll of remembrance before God concerning you and me. Let us all grow together.

Reflection

> The farmer had to feed the tares along with the wheat until fruition for the sake of his wheat. Ask the Holy Spirit for the grace to endure and not to prematurely abort a vision that has some thorns attached to it. Pray for grace to keep your focus on the glory and the good ahead of you.

Further reading:

Matthew 13.

Day 4
Submission to God

"Those who belong to Christ Jesus have crucified the flesh with its passions and desires."

Galatians 5:24

Belonging to Christ means being Christ's in our entirety, not partially and not as and when we please. Being Christ's therefore requires a total surrender of ourselves to the will and character of Christ.

This is where we come to the difficult part - to crucify our flesh with the affections and lusts. You and I will appreciate the fact that crucifixion is a very painful way of death. It is a slow, painful and a shameful way to die. But this is exactly how God wants our flesh to die - we must crucify our flesh.

The flesh is anything that is contrary to the character of God. Pride, insecurity, selfishness, ingratitude, to name but a few, are all embedded in us naturally. It is normal and sometimes cultural to be proud especially if your lineage has earthly royalty. So members of royal families all over the world are accorded some form of respect and homage thus ranking them above commoners. These traits are in our ordinary day to day lives but when we become born again, we enter a new kingdom where things are different.

We live in the flesh but when we submit to the Spirit of God in us, the Spirit takes control. The scripture points us to the need to submit our flesh and desires to the leading of the Word of God and to the Holy Spirit. It's only when we measure ourselves against God's standards that we get to know where we are!

> *"We do not dare to classify or compare ourselves with some who commend themselves. When they measure themselves by themselves and compare themselves with themselves, they are not wise."*
> 2 Corinthians 10:12

And may I submit to you that God's standards are not the same as man's standards. They are bigger, better, and higher than ours. They also look different from ours. What man approves may be totally different from what God approves.

Consequently, dear friend, the Bible is telling us to *"crucify our flesh with its passions and desires"*. Does that give us a responsibility? Yes. Do we have to work for our salvation? No, but I do know the onus is on us. If we do not yield to the Spirit, our flesh will take over and if our flesh takes over then we're not Christ's and if we're not Christ's then whose are we?

Reflection

> Submit every affection or that which you feel - anger, resentment, pain and every lust or that which you crave, revenge, covetousness and self-aggrandizement - to Christ.
>
> Let the Holy Spirit guide your emotions and your mind. Don't give Him a part and hold on to the other part. Give Him everything because *"those that are led by the Spirit of God, they are the sons of God."* Romans 8:14

Further Reading:

Galatians 5.

Day 5
Play Your Part (1)

"But he did not consummate their marriage until she gave birth to a son. And he gave him the name Jesus."

Matthew 1:25

Fruitfulness is first and foremost knowing your role and executing it well. To birth any great vision, the bearers of it need to come together and work in complete harmony to successfully deliver the vision. I would like to compare this to the role of a father and a mother in a home. Mary was the bearer of the vision. She carried the vision in her body for nine months but Joseph had a role to play as well. He protected the vision.

Joseph did not consummate their marriage because something bigger and greater was at stake. I'm yet to come across a young man who can wait for nine months after marriage to consummate the marriage. Consummating the marriage would have defiled the holy seed so Joseph protected the vision by waiting. I am led to believe that Joseph was a virgin otherwise he would have burned with sexual desire but he sacrificed his emotions and pride as a man to protect the vision that Mary carried.

If you're a man, your role is to protect your family as the head of the family. But before you can do that, you'll have to come to the realisation that you carry the destinies of the people in your nuclear family. Your wife and your children are under your divine authority just as Mary and the baby Jesus were under Joseph's authority. You have a heavenly responsibility to protect your family physically and spiritually – spiritually, by praying and interceding for them.

Three times in the passage, we read that the angel of the Lord appeared to Joseph in a dream:

> *"But after he had considered this, an angel of the Lord appeared to him in a dream and said, 'Joseph, son of David, do not be afraid to take Mary home as your wife, because what is conceived in her is from the Holy Spirit.'"*

> *"When they had gone, an angel of the Lord appeared to Joseph in a dream. 'Get up,' he said, 'take the child and his mother and escape to Egypt. Stay there until I tell you, for Herod is going to search for the child to kill him...' After Herod died, an angel of the Lord appeared in a dream to Joseph in Egypt."*
> Matthew 1:20; 2:13 & 19

We can therefore infer that Joseph was a man who submitted to God. To fulfil your role as the man, father and/or husband, it is important to submit to God Almighty. Make Him your source, and respect the Lord as your Head.

Reflection

Submit to Christ and take on your role as the protector of what God has entrusted into your care. Pray for your wife and your children. Ask the Lord to show you ways to support them and help you.

Further Reading:

1 Corinthians 11.

Day 6

Play Your Part (2)

"But Jael, Heber's wife, picked up a tent peg and a hammer and went quietly to him while he lay fast asleep, exhausted. She drove the peg through his temple into the ground, and he died."

Judges 4:21

Judges chapter 4 summarises the life of the children of Israel after the death of Joshua. They were now in the promised land but meddling in sin and everything contrary to what God had instructed of them. As a result, they were overthrown by the neighbouring nations and oppressed for twenty good years.

They cried out to God for deliverance. His plan had three major characters: Deborah, a prophetess and a judge of Israel, Barak the military general and Jael, a housewife or a home maker in modern terms. The enemy, Sisera - the captain of the Canaanite army, had 900 chariots. The chariots of iron in those times were intimidating and the most advanced technological weapon. Deborah gave Barak a prophetic direction regarding God's deliverance, but he put his own conditions on the word of God before agreeing to it.

Jael, a housewife, was home when Sisera came to her for shelter. The battle was fierce, and the captain had left the battle to have a nap! Jael knew the implications of the battle, that there would be peace and prosperity for Israel if Sisera was dead. She took a tent peg which was like a big nail and drove it right through his temple.

We see here, a woman, not a warrior, who managed to slay the fiercest army commander in her time for the deliverance of the people of God, Jael was available and

God used her.

No matter who you are and what you have, if you avail yourself, the Lord can use you to do great feats. Jael was in her house at the right time to be able to offer hospitality to Sisera. If she had been visiting a friend or out and about, she would have missed an opportunity to be used by the Lord. We must be discerning enough to be at the right place, at the right time to be a tool in God's hands.

The Lord does not need much, he only needs us to be there, exactly where he wants us because the ability to do whatever he wants us to do will come from Him. Imagine, a woman driving a tent peg through a man's temple. She could have only done it because the Lord gave her the strength to do it.

Play your part, be at the right place at the right time and you'll be amazed what the Lord will do through you, no matter the resources you have. This 'insignificant' housewife was needed in God's deliverance plan for Israel. Deborah, Barack and Jael will always be remembered. Do not underestimate your significance in the Lord's agenda.

Reflection

> Ask the Lord for wisdom and grace not to leave your post, whether in your career, marriage, parenting or ministry. You're serving the Lord's purpose and things will not be the same without you.

Further Reading:

> Judges 4.

Day 7
God's Shelter

"They answered: 'Your servants have come from a very distant country because of the fame of the Lord your God. For we have heard reports of him: all that he did in Egypt, and all that he did to the two kings of the Amorites east of the Jordan - Sihon king of Heshbon, and Og king of Bashan, who reigned in Ashtaroth. And our elders and all those living in our country said to us, 'Take provisions for your journey; go and meet them and say to them, - We are your servants; make a treaty with us.'"
Joshua 9:9-11

The Gibeonites lived not too far from the Israelites. They had heard of how the Israelites had conquered the other nations mightier than them on the way to the promised land. The Israelites were ravaging the nations on the way to Canaan and the Gibeonites were next in line. They perceived that they were coming for them in full force so they devised a plan. They couldn't conquer the Israelites so they decided to form an alliance.

How they went about it is another issue for discussion, but their motive was noticeably clear. They had heard of the fame of the Lord and had come to make a treaty with the people of God!

What do you do when you hear great things being said about another company or church, taking over bulldozers in the industry? Do you prepare yourself for a losing battle? Do you prepare to be a losing competitor? Or do you just give up and get ready to be vanquished? The Gibeonites were at a make or break point. They knew they could not fight the Israelites and they knew they could not just sit and wish the impending calamity away. They had to do something. And most importantly, they recognised that it was the Lord God fighting for the Israelites.

Success without God is not good success - see Joshua 1:8. But when you recognise good success, beloved, run towards and embrace it. It will teach you a thing or two if you're ready to learn. Lot prospered because of Abraham. Divine location is important and that's exactly what the Gibeonites did. They made an alliance with the Israelites and became their servants.

The truth is the Gibeonites, a pagan nation, had made a treaty with God and not just Israel. That treaty changed their destiny as a nation and up to this day, they are counted among Israel.

The Lord our God is Jehovah Almighty. Align with Him and have good success. He has all provision, protection and power in His hands. In Him you'll have peace, your dreams will be realised, and you'll have eternal life. Don't resist him, you'll be fighting a losing battle. Make an alliance with him, you'll not be disappointed.

Reflection

> If you don't know or if you have strayed from Jesus, you cannot be fruitful by yourself. *"For in him we live and move and have our being."* (Acts 17:28)

Further reading:

Joshua 10.

Day 8

God's Leading

" 'Lord,' Ananias answered, 'I have heard many reports about this man and all the harm he has done to your holy people in Jerusalem. And he has come here with authority from the chief priests to arrest all who call on your name." But the Lord said to Ananias, 'Go! This man is my chosen instrument to proclaim my name to the Gentiles and their kings and to the people of Israel.'"

Acts 9:13-15

A disciple in the early church had an instruction from God. He would have been in these modern times a 'normal' Christian like you and me. The only reason why we know about him is because of a bold step he took. And we're going to look further into this disciple.

The Lord appeared to Ananias and asked him to go, find and pray for a notorious new convert. Someone who had been an enemy of the faith. This was during the persecution of the early Christians in Acts chapter 8. They had already been chased out of their city and had to start life all over again seeking asylum elsewhere. And just when things seemed to be calming down, the Lord told him, *"go and meet Saul"*, the man who chased you out of Jerusalem, the man who was present during Stephen's death. Go and lay your hands on him. He's blind but if you lay your hand on him, and pray for him, his eyes will be opened.

For me, this would have been a catch 22 situation. Lord! Are you being serious? It's good that he's blind. Maybe we should leave him blind, that way he won't be able to make life unbearable for all of us!

Are there times when you feel the Lord is leading you into danger? When you think you've just survived one storm, He tends to lead you into another one?

If only we'd come to God with our doubts and fears, He'd speak to us and show us the bigger picture. When we take our eyes off ourselves, and realise how we fit into the bigger picture, it's easier to walk in obedience. Obedience to God, every single directive from God, is essential towards a victorious, fruitful Christian life.

Eventually, there was permanent safety for the church as a result of Ananias' obedience. They increased in numbers and everyone enjoyed peace after the conversion of Paul. The church had rest.

Could it be that the Lord had already spoken to a few people who had refused to go before He spoke to Ananias? I don't know but what I do know is that whenever the Lord is pulling you out of your comfort zone, He has something bigger than you in the pipeline - see Jeremiah 29:11.

All we have to do is follow His lead. Faith is obedience and obedience is faith.

Reflection

> Is the Lord asking you to do something which is out of your depth? Is He pulling you out of your comfort zone? You can totally trust Him.

Further Reading:

> Acts 9.

Day 9

The Paths of Righteousness

"He restores my soul; He leads me in the paths of righteousness For His name's sake."
Psalms 23:3 NKJV

In this popular scripture, the Psalmist tells of how the Lord gives us restoration: by leading us in the paths of righteousness. We can therefore infer that restoration comes when the Lord leads us in the paths of righteousness.

The first question to ask is restoration into what? Secondly, what does this path look like? Firstly, restoration to our original image as in His image. Restoration back to God's original intention when He created man. We were meant to be like Him, to have dominion and to live forever. Therefore, for God to achieve this restoration of our original state, he uses the process of His leading and our obedience into the paths of righteousness.

Now to our second question - what do the paths of righteousness look like to you? And most importantly, what does this process look like to God? In order to go through this restoration process, the one being taken and the one providing the leadership must be in agreement. You must be on the same page with God to walk that path when he leads you. It is not a matter of if he will, but rather a matter of our following his lead.

The right paths is a pruning, moulding and healing process for every believer. It might look different on an individual basis, but the outcome is the same for you and me, that is - to restore us back to God. It may be long winded, it may need patience, it may need our character refined and our motives re-calibrated but it's all to His glory. The purpose of the process is to take away every iota of self so that we can learn to put our hope, strength and trust totally in and on God.

> *"Then he said to them all: 'Whoever wants to be my disciple must deny themselves and take up their cross daily and follow me.'"*
>
> *Luke 9:23*

That seems a bit harsh for Jesus to say, after the disciples had left everything to follow him. But our Lord was hitting the nail right on the head that following him was a journey of self-denial and transformation. It is a journey of going through the mill to be churned till all the chaff in us is sifted out. To be like Christ, so we may be fruitful and that our fruits may remain.

> *"You did not choose me, but I chose you and appointed you so that you might go and bear fruit—fruit that will last—and so that whatever you ask in my name the Father will give you."*
>
> *John 15:16*

Reflection

Commit yourself to the Lord and ask for his grace his transforming grace in every stage of your life so that you can be more like Him - dependable, loving, compassionate, truthful and a carrier of His presence.

Further Reading:

Psalm 23.

Day 10

Discretion

> *"Esther had not revealed her nationality and family background, because Mordecai had forbidden her to do so."*
>
> Esther 2:10

In the book of Esther, we read about the life of a young, orphan girl who rose from poverty to the palace. This beautiful story lays out God's deliverance master plan for His people. The young girl Esther was taken into the company of brides-to-be for the King. Taken from her only relative Mordecai, into an unfamiliar territory with non-Jewish women.

From experience whenever one goes to an unfamiliar environment, the first advice is to make friends and share experiences so one can blend in and be comfortable. Esther did the exact opposite, she stayed in the harem for 12 full months and no one knew her family or background.

Without doubt, those would have been the first pleasantries to be exchanged as soon as she arrived in the harem but Esther didn't tow that path. She was there to fulfil a heavenly assignment. She was there not as a beauty queen but as an ambassador for the Jewish community. Lives and a generation depended on her.

> *"Those who consider themselves religious and yet do not keep a tight rein on their tongues deceive themselves, and their religion is worthless."*
>
> James 1:26

The scripture above puts it perfectly well. As Christ's ambassadors, with the assignment of soul winning, we must be on the field without exposing and aborting the assignment for which we were sent. Too much talk and telling will abort the purpose.

> *"Even fools are thought wise if they keep silent, and discerning if they hold their tongues."*
>
> Proverbs 17:28

Beloved, learn to hold your tongue. Don't talk too much. Some of us can divulge secrets within minutes, family secrets, company plans and career plans. We give the enemy an advantage when we talk too much. Imagine if the King had known that Esther was a Jew? She would have been disqualified from the pageant because the Jews were slaves in Persia and I'm sure the King would not have chosen a slave queen.

You're where you are for a divine purpose. Focus on the assignment, excel in everything you do. At the right time, the Lord will elevate you and show you forth just as Esther was shown forth after her assignment. The truth is she was a Jew whether or not people knew. You are who you are whether people know about you or not. People not knowing does not make you less of who you are.

Reflection

Pray and ask the Lord for grace to say the right thing at the right time.

Further Reading:

James 3.

Day 11

Honouring our Parents

"Jesus replied, 'And why do you break the command of God for the sake of your tradition? For God said, 'Honour your father and mother' and 'Anyone who curses their father or mother is to be put to death.' But you say that if anyone declares that what might have been used to help their father or mother is 'devoted to God,' they are not to 'honour their father or mother' with it. Thus, you nullify the word of God for the sake of your tradition."
Matthew 15:3-6

The Pharisees had Jesus on their radar because he was constantly challenging their reputation and motives. In this scripture Jesus raises an important standard for fruitfulness - "honour your father and mother". Honouring our parents consists of loving and respecting them in totality whether they're good or bad, and to not saying a negative word about them. Secondly, it means meeting their needs - needs, not wants.

To avoid with the responsibility, the Pharisees decided that instead of giving to their parents, they would give the money to God - they called it 'corban' (Mark 7:11). Thus they thought no one could hold them responsible for not honouring their parents as God was considered the priority. Jesus rebuked them for this reckless behaviour.

I know not all parental relationships may be positive. Some parents exert forceful parental authority such that when children become adults, they don't want to have anything to do with them. But as children of God, we can in no way not pick and choose what to obey and what not to obey from the Word of God.

> *"Honour your father and mother" - which is the first commandment with a promise - "so that it may go well with you and that you may enjoy long life on the earth."*
>
> Ephesians 6:2-3

Honouring our parents comes with a promise of long life.

No matter our relationship with our parents, be it biological or not, we owe them a responsibility in the eyes of God to honour them. Otherwise, God will call us hypocrites just as Jesus described the Pharisees. It does not matter how much we give to God and others. It does not matter how much offering or tithes we give. We have a responsibility not to be bitter against them or speak derogatorily of them. If we ignore our parents and do not take care of them, or dishonour them, we are in transgression of His Word and will be denied the promise of Ephesians 6:2.

You honour God by honouring your parents. It will be well with you and you will enjoy long life.

Reflection

> Is there a difficult past you need to surrender? Do you need to forgive your parents for something in the past? Ask the Holy Spirit to help you release every pain and hurt to Him. Ask the Lord to give you grace to be generous towards any parental figure in your life.

Further Reading:

> Ephesians 6.

Day 12

Proved by the Word

"They bruised his feet with shackles, his neck was put in irons, till what he foretold came to pass, till the word of the Lord proved him true."

Psalms 105:18-19

In the book of Genesis, almost 10 chapters are dedicated to the young man Joseph, the eleventh son of Jacob. Joseph had a calling on his life to deliver his family from famine and death. He was called to be the provider and protector of his father's offspring. Remember Jacob carried the Abrahamic blessing and God needed to partner with someone from the seed of Jacob to ensure His plan and word concerning Abraham's descendants would happen just as planned.

For such a huge responsibility, God needed someone manageable whom He could trust and rely on. Joseph had to undergo seventeen years of "proving" as the Bible describes it.

I believe the Word of God proved Joseph just as we do with dough. You knead the dough thoroughly and leave it to rest. In the resting process, the dough rises to give a perfect consistency when baked. If the dough is not proven well, the pastry may not turn out exactly right.

Beloved, our Lord Jesus walked the surface of this earth for thirty years before embarking on a ministry that lasted only three years. He learnt to live fully as a man and *"Son though He was, He learned obedience from what He suffered and, once made perfect, He became the source of eternal salvation for all who obey Him."* (Hebrews 5:8-9)

For you to be fruitful in life, you have to go through your

"proving" process. For some of us, God may have to prove us so that He can totally depend on us when it comes to our money and wealth. This is how we know that it is not ours but God's, channelled through us. For some of us, it's our ego - we think either too highly or too lowly of ourselves. God may have to spend some quality time shaping us in that area.

Would you give a knife to an infant? In the same way, our Lord will not put great responsibility in the hands of an irresponsible person. If you're not proved, you may not even realise the burden of the responsibility.

Reflection

> Allow the Holy Spirit to do a good work in your life; a half-baked cake is not good to anyone. Allow God to shape you and when the set time comes, He'll glorify you. If you give the glory back to Him, you'll understand that it was not about you in the first place, but about the lives and souls that needed to be saved. You will look back and thank God for the opportunity to have been be the chosen vessel.

Further Reading:

> Psalm 105.

Day 13

Partnership

"Adam and his wife were both naked, and they felt no shame."

Genesis 2:25

"In the beginning, God created the heaven and the earth" (Genesis 1:1). He made man and woman and put them in charge of all that He had created. He put these two people in charge over the land and everything on it, the sea and everything in it and the sky and everything in it. He gave them dominion - *"God blessed them and said to them, 'Be fruitful and increase in number; fill the earth and subdue it. Rule over the fish in the sea and the birds in the sky and over every living creature that moves on the ground.'"* (Genesis 1:28)

Adam and his wife were both naked, and they felt no shame. To be able to exercise your dominion mandate, you must be able to be vulnerable before your spouse and not be embarrassed. There must be complete transparency and accountability. Adam and Eve were exposed to each other yet felt no shame.

You may not be ready for a victorious marriage if you have an issue bearing it all before your spouse. In the same way, if you have trust issues, you may not be ready for the dominion- taking marriage.

This principle is equally true for any partnership, whether business or ministerial. *"Do two walk together unless they have agreed to do so?"* (Amos 3:3)

A partnership can not stand unless there's total transparency and accountability. The great responsibility of taking dominion over the earth demanded a strong partnership between Adam and Eve. But we have an even more dependable helper, the Holy Spirit, to help us strengthen our relationship and to hold on to each other through thick and thin.

To be "naked" with your spouse means to keep standing strong despite any hurt or pains, to keep ploughing on no matter the disappointments and to keep focused on the purpose at stake. We all know how the story went - after some time, Eve ate the fruit and gave to Adam to eat too. They showed serious contempt for the instructions of God, but they kept their relationship. They stayed together, weathered the storm, had children, raised them up, encountered serious parental issues but did not abandon each other. Together they took care of everything God had given them charge of. You and I are here today because of their commitment.

Reflection

> Be transparent with your business partners, and totally honest in your partnerships. Without total honesty and commitment, no partnership will succeed but the Lord has ordained that some victories are sweeter and quicker when we work in partnership. *"How could one man chase a thousand, or two put ten thousand to flight?"* (Deuteronomy 32:30)

Further Reading:

> 1 Corinthians 12.

Day 14

If Not Sure

" '... whoever blasphemes against the Holy Spirit will never be forgiven; they are guilty of an eternal sin." He said this because they were saying, 'He has an impure spirit.'"

Mark 3:29-30

We live in times where all men claim to be spiritual. We can be spiritual towards God or spiritual towards the signs and the subtle manipulations of the devil. People are having experiences that they cannot explain - strange, out-of-body experiences, and the quest for knowledge has overwhelmed our world.

In all these, God is still working. He is still doing signs and wonders in the lives of His people. He's still working miracles with and through His people. The trouble is, how do you know it's God?

Jesus experienced a similar circumstance during His time. At the start of His ministry, people didn't know what to make of Him; even His own family were not sure him. They were double minded about whether to receive His ministry or not, to the extent that *"When His family heard about this, they went to take charge of Him, for they said, 'He is out of His mind.'"* (Mark 3:21) They went to talk Him out of His ministry publicly because they weren't sure that it was God working in and through Him.

Beloved, let us be careful to discern the Spirit of God otherwise we'll risk eternal damnation.

You'll bear witness that there are numerous prophets, pastors, apostles and men of God in our days - some with big titles and some without. Some are controversial and cause us to question the workings of the Spirit. Some come in rough packaging with lots of excesses, but in all these God is still at work in and through His chosen ones.

Be sure before you judge. Be sure before you say anything against anybody. Gamaliel told the council, *"'Therefore, in the present case I advise you: Leave these men alone! Let them go! For if their purpose or activity is of human origin, it will fail. But if it is from God, you will not be able to stop these men; you will only find yourselves fighting against God."* (Acts 5:38-39)

If the source is God, it will endure the test of time. If otherwise, it will fall and crumble. Time will tell. If we associate the work and the stirrings of God to the devil, we commit a blasphemy against the Holy Spirit.

Jesus did not come packaged as the 'King' the Israelites were expecting. Hence, they fought and resisted Him. God is unpredictable. Out of the chaos and darkness, the Spirit of the Lord is hovering over his chosen ones. I hope you are one of them.

Reflection

> Pray that the Lord will open your eyes to see when He's working in your life. Ask that he speaks to you in his still, small voice. Pray for revelational knowledge to discern the hand of God.

Further Reading:

> Mark 3.

Day 15

Right from Home

> *"But you will receive power when the Holy Spirit comes on you; and you will be my witnesses in Jerusalem, and in all Judea and Samaria, and to the ends of the earth."*
>
> Acts 1:8

Right from the start of His ministry, I believe this was exactly what Jesus was trying to tell His disciples before His departure. The message was - Start from home, when you receive the power of the Holy Spirit, let the transformation in you begin from your home. Start right where you live, where you are known, around the people you love and who love you. You must be my witness in Jerusalem before you move out to the outskirts of Judea.

We are often tempted to be more nice and polite to people outside than with the people close to us. We might be overly harsh with our children, with our spouses than we would with people at work or at church. The excuse is that they live with us so are permitted to see our true self. The question then is what is your true self?

Clearly, it is not what your friends see, not what your work colleagues see nor what you portray when in church. So, what is your true self? Is your true self a reflection of Jesus? Paul gave a criteria for choosing an overseer as someone who *"... must manage his own family well and see that his children obey him, and he must do so in a manner worthy of full respect. (If anyone does not know how to manage his own family, how can he take care of God's church?)"* (1 Timothy 3:4-5)

To "manage... in a manner worthy of full respect" means being respectful to our children, our spouses and the people we live with, as well as our closest acquaintances. If we won't portray a particular attitude to outsiders, then our immediate family are also good enough not to be at the receiving end. Anger, rage, violence and passive aggression just to mention a few are behaviours that become engrained in us with time and therefore don't go away overnight. Pray and ask the Holy Spirit to help you break free from the hold of Satan and seek professional counsel if needed.

We cannot build on a wobbly foundation, otherwise eventually everything will come tumbling down. In the same way, we cannot hide some negative behaviours in our closets and profess Christ outside. Effective witnessing starts with our families and immediate friends. Let them see that Christ really dwells in us, let them be our first witnesses. And trust me, our faith will be tested by the ones we love in so many ways. If we can pass the test of family, we'll really pass the test of ministry and purpose.

Reflection

> Is there a relationship you might need to repair? Be honest about what has gone wrong, ask for forgiveness and take that step towards reconciliation.

Further reading:

> 2 Peter 1.

Day 16

Faith Does

> *"Gideon and the hundred men with him reached the edge of the camp at the beginning of the middle watch, just after they had changed the guard. They blew their trumpets and broke the jars that were in their hands. The three companies blew the trumpets and smashed the jars. Grasping the torches in their left hands and holding in their right hands the trumpets they were to blow, they shouted, 'A sword for the Lord and for Gideon!' While each man held his position around the camp, all the Midianites ran, crying out as they fled."*
>
> Judges 7:19-21

A trumpet, a clay jar and a torch. These were the weapons in the hands of the three hundred soldiers that went out to war against a Midianite army of one hundred and thirty five thousand.

Call it crazy, but that was exactly God's plan. God's plan was to do what was impossible. And to be part of God's plan, we just have to grab the bull by the horns and be all in or fully out.

Gideon was caught in between; I suppose he had no choice after twenty-two thousand of his men admitted blatantly that they were fearful. Then a further nine thousand seven hundred were sent home by God. Reduced from thirty-two thousand men to just three hundred! To make matters worse, God says take a clay jar, a trumpet and a torchlight to set up your ambush!

Beloved, faith does. Faith responds to the word of God,

every word of God. Faith is required for a victorious Christian life. If we take the step in faith, God will sort the rest out. We may not know how or when but He'll surely do it.

The account tells how the men stood still after blowing their trumpets, breaking their jars and giving a shout. They stood still and watched the enemy turn on one another out of panic - *"... the Lord caused the men throughout the camp to turn on each other with their swords. The army fled ... "* (Judges 7:22)

After you have moved in faith, stand still and see the work of the Lord. Stand still and let God do His thing. If He doesn't do what He has promised, then His reputation will be at stake. He reasssured Job, *"So listen to me, you men of understanding. Far be it from God to do evil, from the Almighty to do wrong."* (Job 34:10)

If God can turn things around for Gideon and his men, He can surely do the same for you in any situation. Just trust him with your clay jar, your trumpet and your torch. Trust Him with whatever is in your hands, no matter how impossible it is. Faith in God means doing what He says. Just do it. *"In the same way, faith by itself, if it is not accompanied by action, is dead."* (James 2:17)

Reflection

> Is there a desperate situation on your hands? Do you have a direction from God? Step out in faith and do exactly what God has told you.

Further Reading:

> Judges 7.

Day 17

Pursuing the Lord's Agenda

> *"Now when Joshua was near Jericho, he looked up and saw a man standing in front of him with a drawn sword in his hand. Joshua went up to him and asked, 'Are you for us or for our enemies?' 'Neither,' he replied, 'but as commander of the army of the Lord I have now come.' Then Joshua fell face-down to the ground in reverence, and asked him, 'What message does my Lord have for his servant?' The commander of the Lord's army replied, 'Take off your sandals, for the place where you are standing is holy.' And Joshua did so."*
>
> Joshua 5:13-15

Israel was about to face a great city in battle. Jericho was well fortified. They were moving to a land of the unknown with strong cities and kings to contend with.

When Joshua was near Jericho, he lifted his eyes and saw a deity whom the Bible describes as 'Captain of the Lord's army'.

Beloved, God is with us at every present moment. He does not leave us by ourselves. And now and again, He opens our eyes to see Him so our faith does not wane.

The captain of the Lord's army stands in front of Joshua and Joshua speaks first - *" are you for us or against us?"* But the Lord answered and said "neither, but as commander of the Lord's army I have come." The pre-incarnate Christ said - I'm not on your side or your enemy's side. I am on the Lord's side so you choose whose side you want to be on.

Joshua then bowed down and worshipped, thereby

confirming which side he was on. The destruction of Jericho was the Lord's agenda and He was ready to work with anyone on His side. Before that, Joshua must have thought that Jericho was his enemy but after he aligned with the Lord, he came to realise that Jericho was 'a piece of cake'. They did not have to draw a sword to pull down the fortified walls of Jericho. The walls came down with a shout - a common shout.

Complications can be unravelled easily when we are on the Lord's side. We have to position ourselves not to take the responsibility that is God's, but to follow His direction and His plan. Pursue the Lord's agenda.

Reflection

Are you in line with the Lord in your family, career, ministry or even personal finances? Do you know God's plan for where you are right now in your life's journey? If you don't - find it, and if you do already, pursue that agenda faithfully. Ask the Lord to help you to be faithful to His plans for you.

Further Reading:

Joshua 6.

Day 18

Contending for the Faith

"Dear friends, although I was very eager to write to you about the salvation we share, I felt compelled to write and urge you to contend for the faith that was once for all entrusted to God's holy people."

Jude 1:3

To contend for something is normally used in the negative sense. Aggression and contention are not two qualities that we would normally associate with children of God unless we consider the purpose of the aggression.

In the scripture above, the apostle urged the beloved to contend for the faith; in other words, to fight for, defend and guard the faith that has been entrusted to them. 2 Peter 1:1 describes our faith in Christ as "precious".

Beloved to be fruitful, you and I must hold on to our faith in Christ as precious gold. Our faith in Christ has a promise of reward here on earth and eternal life after death.

"And everyone who has left houses or brothers or sisters or father or mother or wife or children or fields for my sake will receive a hundred times as much and will inherit eternal life."

Matthew 19:29

Contending for your faith can include staying away from friendships that do not build you up; keeping your mind set on Christ; keeping your eye on the goal before you; watching out for character traits here and there that defile and contaminate you; and avoiding conversations that cause you to water down and compromise your faith. You know the weaker links in your fortress that need extra security.

Our faith is worth fighting for, your faith in Christ is worth contending for. There are people waiting to snatch what you have from you if you do not guard it with all diligence. There is someone waiting to take your job if you slack in it, there is someone waiting to take your place if you don't hold on to what you have. The enemy can make you replace your genuine jewel with a fake one and he will try to get you to compromise subtly till you have got nothing left.

Contend for your faith, family, career, and your life. Your life is worth living for, no matter the highs and the lows. Don't take whatever is in your hands and in your life for granted. That job has a future and that marriage is a power alliance in its formation stage. You stand for the righteousness of God; therefore contend for the faith that has been entrusted to you.

Reflection

> Is there any area of your life that you may have exposed to the wrong person? What have you taken for granted? Bring it before the Lord in prayer and ask the Holy Spirit to help you diligently guard your faith and all that He has entrusted into your care.

Further Reading:

> Jude 1.

Day 19

Abiding in Him (1)

"Lot and his two daughters left Zoar and settled in the mountains, for he was afraid to stay in Zoar. He and his two daughters lived in a cave."

Genesis 19:30

Once again, we look at the story of Lot. I find Lot an intriguing character because his life makes me ponder a lot of things.

Adopted at a tender age, he was raised and mentored by his uncle Abraham. Lot became rich, had servants and livestock to the point that he could no longer co-exist with his uncle. It does not appear from the scripture that Lot ever sat down and assessed why the Lord was blessing him; he never realised that it was only because he was following Abraham. Abraham was the one the Lord called from the Land of Ur (Genesis 12:1-5). He was the one who carried the promise of the blessing, he was the one on a journey to the unknown. Lot benefited from the Lord's blessing by virtue of his association with Abraham and not because the Lord had called him. Lot's wealth was dependent on Abraham's obedience to God, yet here he was, a young man making plans and dreams of becoming bigger than his uncle.

Lot chose the better land with water although both Abraham and he needed water for their livestock (Genesis 13:9-12). He moved away from Abraham into a well-watered land and gradually pitched his tent in Sodom and Gomorrah.

In Genesis 14, he was rescued by Abraham from the hands of five kings. In chapters 18 and 19 we see yet again Abraham interceding for the rescue of Lot from danger.

After the first rescue you would wonder why Lot did not return to Abraham but continued staying in Sodom? After this second rescue, still Lot was determined to stay in the small city of Zoar, away from Abraham.

By the end of the chapter, this righteous man had fathered two sons with his own daughters.

Beloved, no matter the point we must prove, Christ is our source, our shield and our supply.

> *"For you know the grace of our Lord Jesus Christ, that though he was rich, yet for your sake he became poor, so that you through his poverty might become rich."*
>
> 2 Corinthians 8:9

We cannot thrive outside of our source. Lot lost everything because he moved away from the source of his blessing. *"Remain in me, as I also remain in you. No branch can bear fruit by itself; it must remain in the vine. Neither can you bear fruit unless you remain in me."* (John 15:4)

Reflection

Are you where the Lord wants you to be? Reflect on the various aspects of your life. Ask the Lord to give you the grace to make up with any godly associations with whom you may have severed ties. Ask the Holy Spirit to give you the grace to be in His will at every point in time.

Further Reading:

Genesis 19.

Day 20

Abiding in Him (2)

"I am the vine, you are the branches. He who abides in Me, and I in him, bears much fruit; for without Me you can do nothing."

John 15:5

The book of Ruth is a story that epitomises divine location. Chapter 1 tells the journey of Elimelech from Bethlehem to the country of Moab. The Moabites did not worship God, they were a pagan nation but Elimelech moved his family away from the presence of God in search of greener pastures.

While in Moab, we read of the tragedy that befell that family. They lost all the males in the family and Naomi, his wife, decides to return to Bethlehem. Ruth, the Moabitess daughter in-law of Naomi, decides to return with Naomi. She was not an Israelite, but she relocated from Moab to join the people of God because of her mother in-law.

Beloved, God is the source of every good thing and everything that we need. Naomi returned to her people and the land was in plenty. Ruth carved a new destiny for herself by aligning with the people of God.

Your location is vital to your fruitfulness. Do not remove yourself from your divine location because of some temporary setback or chaos. God's got you on His agenda. Do not dislocate yourself from His presence, do not remove yourself from His covering.

Often, we make a premature move only to miss our *kairos* (God's timing) moment - the day of our visitation. Naomi moved away and lost everything, all that she was searching for was realised when she returned to Bethlehem. Ruth did not have anything, but she found peace, purpose, and prosperity when she grafted herself into Naomi's divine location.

Do you know your divine location? Is it your marriage? Is it your ministry? Could it be through that failing career that God will use you to transform the world? Could it be through that child that God will raise the next world changer? Don't abandon your position. Jesus admonished His disciples that *"... apart from me you can do nothing."* (John 15:5).

> *"The righteous will flourish like a palm tree, they will grow like a cedar of Lebanon; planted in the house of the Lord, they will flourish in the courts of our God. They will still bear fruit in old age, they will stay fresh and green, proclaiming, 'The Lord is upright; He is my Rock, and there is no wickedness in Him.'"*
>
> Psalms 92:12-15

Reflection

There's no unrighteousness in God. Ask for grace to keep abiding where He wants you to be and to redirect you back to your divine location in case you are not there.

Further Reading:

Ruth 1.

Day 21

The Extra Oil

"The foolish ones said to the wise, 'Give us some of your oil; our lamps are going out.'"

Matthew 25:8

The story of the ten virgins is a popular one. Ten virgins prepared to meet the groom, the groom tarried and in the waiting period, life happened and they slept. All of them slept, they were all exposed to similar conditions of life. But in the middle of the night, there was a wake-up call and they had to get up to answer to the purpose of their wait: the groom had arrived! The time for reward was here! The long awaited expectation was now a reality.

Beloved, in our journey of life, there will be a moment of reckoning. This is when we will be placed on a scale and have to answer for what we have done with the resources the Lord has given us. These virgins were aware of the journey ahead of them: waiting for the groom. But the Bible says during the wait, they slept. For some of us that will mean getting up the career ladder, getting married, parenting, taking care of extended family, battling with a health issue and the challenges we must surmount in our daily lives.

Life gets in the way, but we don't have to lose focus on the reason why we are here. In that career, relationship, or on that hospital bed, the early wakes and late nights must all be subtle reminders that there is a day when everything will end. Then we'll stand in front of our groom and receive a reward - a commendation, for the wait. As a result, to succeed in the wait of life, we need the deposit of extra 'oil'. Sameness only breeds mediocrity and mediocrity is the enemy of excellence. The extra 'oil' is what will make us different from the person next door.

That's what will make my business stand out and your team the one to join. The extra 'oil' is what will make you stand out despite the challenges of life. That extra attention to detail, that smile for that customer, going out of your way to check that email is sent, turning up slightly early to make sure all is set for an event are some of the things that make us better than our equals. And dare I say, most of the time, these are little things that make a big difference.

The Holy Spirit gives us the grace to keep going on when our human strength has reached the end of its rope. He is our extra oil. He's our strength and wisdom.

> *"He gives strength to the weary and increases the power of the weak. Even youths grow tired and weary, and young men stumble and fall; but those who hope in the Lord will renew their strength. They will soar on wings like eagles; they will run and not grow weary, they will walk and not be faint."*
> *Isaiah 40:29-31*

Reflection

Ask the Holy Spirit to give you grace to keep 'burning' no matter how long the wait.

Further Reading:

Matthew 25.

Day 22

Focus

"Saul told his son Jonathan and all the attendants to kill David. But Jonathan had taken a great liking to David."

1 Samuel 19:1

The first book of Samuel recounts the life of Israel's first king - Saul. He was chosen and much loved, with a few flaws. He heard some women praising his own protégée and was engulfed with envy. As a result, he spent his entire reign, chasing after David. When we read 1 Samuel 19-31, we see a king who has no vision for his nation and people; his only obsession is to destroy one young man who was in his service. He pursued David to destroy him so he could feel secure.

King Saul went from the palace to the plains, caves to mountains, from the city to the forests, chasing after David. He slaughtered a whole city of the priests of God for being nice to David (1 Samuel 22:19). Saul was so obsessed with destroying his enemy that he forgot he had a nation to govern.

He actually put Israel in jeopardy because at one point while on the run chasing after David, the real enemy - the Philistines, invaded Israel (1 Samuel 22:27). All Saul needed was for someone to tell him the whereabouts of David: he would abandon his post and go chasing him with all the fighting men of Israel.

What we can learn from this is that we'll achieve nothing in God's purpose if all we do is chase after our enemies. Rather, we need to focus. Focus on yourself, your purpose, your strengths, and areas for improvement. There are always going to be many enemies and people who we just wish are not around to remind us of our failures. And that was what it was. David was an embodiment of the man Saul would never be. Instead of wishing them away or fighting against them, focus on what you can do with what God has entrusted to you. Don't jeopardise what you have in order to destroy someone. Don't stoop low in order to be on the same level with your enemy.

I've noticed that as a people, we can develop a culture of always being in touch with our painful experiences and holding on to them. Consequently, we end up with our pain and the hurt as our focal point and forget about all the blessings and opportunities around us. Saul pursued David for fifteen years and did nothing for Israel. As the first king of Israel, you would think Saul would have done something memorable, but he didn't. Saul died a horrible death because all he ever thought about was destroying David.

God has put a lot more at your disposal than whoever or whatever you think is obstructing your progress. Focus on what is in front of you. Let your hands and your mind be busy on the field of opportunity and responsibility God has given you. Learn to choose your battles and focus. Don't be distracted.

Reflection

> *"Be sure you know the condition of your flocks, give careful attention to your herds; for riches do not endure forever, and a crown is not secure for all generations."*
> (Proverbs 27:23-24)

Further Reading:

1 Samuel 22.

Day 23

What do you do with Jesus?

"Then the people began to plead with Jesus to leave their region. As Jesus was getting into the boat, the man who had been demon-possessed begged to go with Him."

Mark 5:17-18

In the story above, Jesus had restored the sanity of a notoriously dangerous man in the region of Gangrenes but the process of the deliverance was quite a dramatic one. The evil spirits left the man and entered some animals who were feeding nearby. The animals turned wild and drowned in the sea. The news spread like wildfire and before long all the villagers had gathered around Jesus.

The healed man was there as proof of the power of God but instead, they begged Jesus to leave them.

My question to you is - what do you do with Jesus? Do you say 'Lord, you're all powerful so I submit to you' or do you say 'Lord, you're too powerful so go away from me?'

It happened to Peter as well. *"When Simon Peter saw this, he fell at Jesus' knees and said, 'Go away from me, Lord; I am a sinful man!' For he and all his companions were astonished at the catch of fish they had taken."* (Luke 5:8-9)

Jesus was the answer to what the villagers needed - a deliverer, and the answer to what Peter needed - an instructor. But in both scenarios, they asked Jesus to leave them.

Again, what do you do with an authority greater than you trying to come down to your level? What do you do with a great idea, or a great opportunity? Do you respond by saying this is too much for me, or by embracing it even though you don't know how you will deal with it?

The healed man in the story begged to go with Jesus, he wanted to know more about Him. He wanted to worship Him, but the villagers asked Jesus to leave, probably because of the animals they had lost. Surely if they had considered the healed man, they would have seen Jesus as a source of constructive power but because they may have been thinking of the pigs that had drowned, they perceived Him as a source of destructive power.

Our attitude to life determines who we become; and who we are determines our attitude to life. When Moses saw the fire with the bush still green and not burning, he could have run away out of fear or dismay. He could have interpreted the miracle as an attack on his life, but he went near to see. He embraced it and started a supernatural journey with Jehovah Yahweh.

I love what Jesus said to Peter, *"Don't be afraid; from now on you will fish for people."* (Luke 5:10)

Reflection

> Your life will change if you let Him in. Your life will be turned upside down and around if you allow Jesus to be your Lord. Let Him be in charge, in and through you. Let Him stay, embrace Him.

Further Reading:

> Mark 5.

Day 24

The Sympathisers

> *"He went in and said to them, 'Why all this commotion and wailing? The child is not dead but asleep.' But they laughed at Him. After He put them all out, He took the child's father and mother and the disciples who were with Him, and went in where the child was."*
>
> Mark 5:39-40

A young girl had died, and Jesus was on His way to raise her up. With hindsight, we know that Jesus was going to raise the girl up. The girl's father was desperate for Jesus to raise her up but there is a third category of people here in the story that seemed to have a different agenda: the sympathisers.

In verse 38, Jesus assures Jairus "not to be afraid, but to only believe" so although they hear about the girl's death, Jesus still goes to the house with the hope that the father's faith will feed the miracle they needed.

He gets to the house only to be met by a house full of mourners. He attempts to go where the girl's been laid but the mourners now stop mourning and begin to laugh and ridicule Jesus. Surely, the hope of the girl being raised should have been good news to these same people who were crying at the girl's demise. Or could it be that they did not want the girl raised? Could it be that the girl being raised would make them irrelevant? Obviously, if there's no bad news there will be no need for sympathisers. Verse 40 states that *"they laughed at him"*.

Sometimes, people create relevance for themselves in our lives, to our detriment. They lend us a helping hand only for us to build reliance on them, they console us when we need divine anger to propel us from where we are to the next level. They make us comfortable when the discomfort is what we need to propel us from that situation. They tell us how horrible some people are when those 'horrible' people may be our God-sent alliances.

Jesus' vision was clear - He was going to raise the dead girl up but between him and the girl was this mob of sympathisers resisting him. What do you do when you are close to your vision and have an obstacle right in front of you?

Jesus put the crowd out and kept the people who mattered - her parents and his three disciples. To achieve purpose, we must put out the crowd and keep the right company around us. To receive that miracle, we need the people who matter in our lives. People who do not care will mock and laugh and tell you the situation is hopeless. They will not put you first, they'll put themselves and their gratification before you. Jesus put them out and so should you.

Reflection

> Is there someone in your life who has your back whether you're right or wrong? Ask the Lord for wisdom to deal with such a relationship. Pray and ask the Lord to position the people in your life who will be the helpers you need to achieve your purpose.

Further Reading:

> Proverbs 14.

Day 25

What's In You?

> *"Only do not rebel against the Lord. And do not be afraid of the people of the land, because we will devour them. Their protection is gone, but the Lord is with us. Do not be afraid of them."*
>
> Numbers 14:9

When Moses sent 12 spies to Canaan to spy on the land, they came back with two attitudes. A positive and a negative one - with the majority giving the negative.

They gave Moses this account,

> *"'We went into the land to which you sent us, and it does flow with milk and honey! Here is its fruit. But the people who live there are powerful, and the cities are fortified and very large. We even saw descendants of Anak there.' But the men who had gone up with him said, 'We can't attack those people; they are stronger than we are. We saw the Nephilim there (the descendants of Anak come from the Nephilim). We seemed like grasshoppers in our own eyes, and we looked the same to them.'"*
>
> (Numbers 13:27-28, 31, 33)

The question is why did twelve men with the same nationality and same upbringing see the same situation and interpret it so starkly differently?

We see what is in us. Faith or fear, love or hatred, hope or despair - we will see what is in us. Joshua and Caleb had faith in God's promise and therefore saw the opportunities in the land. They saw a people who were weak, fearful and had no protection. The faith in them gave them a winning perspective but the other ten, out of the fear and doubt saw a hopeless situation.

Sometimes we are not even aware that we are afraid. We know when we have faith but not so much when we have fear. *"... faith comes from hearing the message, and the message is heard through the word about Christ."* (Romans 10:17)

Only faith can displace fear. Fill yourself with the Word of God, be around the right crowd and speak the Word of God to yourself over and over again.

Secondly, is the good worth contending for? All the spies at least agreed that the land was good and overwhelmingly fruitful. Why was this good thing not a tool of motivation for them to overlook the giants? Was the goodness in the land not worth fighting for? After all, they left Egypt because of this land the Lord had promised them.

Do you perceive the good in your life as greater than the 'giants'? The good is worth fighting for. In every mountain of life, there's a promise that is greater than the size of the mountain. Keep your eye on the reward and fight the good fight of faith.

Reflection

> What is worth fighting for in your life? Is it your health, that relationship, that child, that career or that ministry? If it's good enough for the enemy, then it's good enough for you.

Further Reading:

Numbers 13.

Day 26

The Seasons

"There is a time for everything, and a season for every activity under the heavens"
Ecclesiastes 3:1

Creation tells about God in such a beautiful way. The seasons of the year determine how we dress and our way of life. We plan our days based on the seasons and the weather. In the same way, we must be able to discern the time and seasons of our lives and respond appropriately.

Knowing the times and seasons of our lives is key to unlocking fruitfulness in the various areas of our lives. In marriage, there is the honeymoon season, then if children come along, the early parenthood season where you're both young parents dealing with infant sickness and A&E trips for falls and scares. Then you may get to the season when the children begin to read the dynamic between you as a couple and set up power battles so they can get their way. These are just a few seasons that I have been through but they are not exhaustive.

There's a time to speak up and defend your position and a time to hold your peace. A time to submit and a time to protest. Our reactions and judgements to every decision must be based on the season we're in. The seasons determine the results we get, not the input of our resources. There's a season for planting corn and a different season for planting yam.

The seasons in life are different depending on where you are. A rainy season in a particular region of a country may not be the same across other regions of that country. In the same way, the seasons of life may vary among siblings, and families and is different for every person. A friend may be going through a fruitful and prosperous season of their life while another may be going through a season of planting where they must put in a lot of work and wait for a period of germination.

The Bible gives an example of a group of men who understood their time and season.

> "... from Issachar, men who understood the times and knew what Israel should do - 200 chiefs, with all their relatives under their command."
> *1 Chronicles 12:32*

Understanding the time and season of your life will help you be in alignment with God's will. These men understood that it was time for David to be King, so they went over to David to hand over the kingdom to him. They knew that there was no point in establishing Saul's legacy on the throne. They understood the prophecies of Samuel and discerned the times. What season of life are you in right now? What decisions do you have to make in these times?

Reflection

> Reflect on some of the things that are holding you back from being your best. Ask the Lord for discernment to understand what season you're in and what you must do appropriately to make the best of it.

Further Reading:

> Ecclesiastes 8.

Day 27
Overcoming your Own

> *"He then said to me: 'Son of man, go now to the people of Israel and speak my words to them. You are not being sent to a people of obscure speech and strange language, but to the people of Israel - not to many peoples of obscure speech and strange language, whose words you cannot understand. Surely if I had sent you to them, they would have listened to you.'"*
>
> Ezekiel 3:4-6

God calls everyone of us to something - a cause, a purpose and a people. Without a people, there will be no cause. People have been on God's agenda all along.

God called Ezekiel to the people of Israel when they were in captivity during the reign of King Jehoiachin (2 Kings 24 and 2 Chronicles 36). The trouble was that the people were very religious but their hearts were far away from God. They knew all the laws and the customs but performed them as a 'tick box' exercise.

> *"And you, son of man, do not be afraid of them or their words. Do not be afraid, though briers and thorns are all around you and you live among scorpions. Do not be afraid of what they say or be terrified by them, though they are a rebellious people."*
>
> Ezekiel 2:6

God knew how stubborn these people were, but he still sent Ezekiel to them and encouraged him to be courageous. He even tells Ezekiel that he would have been better off if he had been sent to a people whose language he did not understand. God was sending him to his own people but he was warned that they would intimidate him, frustrate and try to silence him. God told him not to be alarmed, but to be courageous and say what He asked him to say. That way he would perform His purpose.

It is often the case that the people who will despise your purpose are your own people. *"And they took offence at him. But Jesus said to them, 'A prophet is not without honour except in his own town and in his own home.'"* (Matthew 13:57)

In starting a business idea, in making any major decision and in acceptance of your call, it is likely that the people who will oppose you the most are people from your own tribe, ethnicity and or race, but don't be discouraged. If you can break through that barrier, you can conquer the world. And just as the Lord said to Ezekiel, He says to you too, *"speak my words to them, do not be afraid of what they say or be terrified by them"*. On so many occasions, in the Bible, the Lord assures us not be afraid. He is with you and is bigger and stronger than the opposition you will face. If you can break the hold over you of your people, culture and ethnicity, you can enjoy fruitfulness in your purpose.

Reflection

> Receive this promise over your life - *"But I will make you as unyielding and hardened as they are. I will make your forehead like the hardest stone, harder than flint. Do not be afraid of them or terrified by them, though they are a rebellious people"* (Ezekiel 3:8-9)

Further Reading:

Ezekiel 2.

Day 28

What's Your Reputation?

> *"Jesus and his disciples went on to the villages around Caesarea Philippi. On the way he asked them, 'Who do people say I am?'"*
>
> *Mark 8:27*

Once in a while it's good to know what people think about you (your reputation). But the most important of all is the opinion of those closest to you - your spouse, children, boss, employees, or pastors.

Jesus asked his disciples their opinion of him. At this time Jesus had become very controversial, popular for both the right and wrong reasons. So he asked what people thought about him and most importantly, what his disciples thought about him.

> *"They replied, 'Some say John the Baptist; others say Elijah; and still others, one of the prophets.' 'But what about you?' he asked. 'Who do you say I am?' Peter answered, 'You are the Messiah.' Jesus warned them not to tell anyone about him."*
>
> *Mark 8:28-30*

It is possible you may be in a marriage and not even know the vision of your spouse. Sometimes there can be confusion, just as we saw with Judas Iscariot - Jesus did not quite meet his expectation of the Messiah. Therefore, to build any vision, it is important that every now and then, you go back to the drawing board and check the vision with those who matter the most. Firstly, be sure they understand the vision. Secondly, ensure you are communicating the vision across well and thirdly, ensure they are still loyal to the vision and understand their role in the vision.

It is no wonder that right after this conversation, Jesus started telling them the conditions of service in verses 34 - 38 to reaffirm their loyalty and brace them for what was to come.

Who does your spouse say you are? Can they explain your drive and passion? Do they understand what drives you? Can they explain what you are trying to achieve and why? The same goes with running any organisation and parenting. We may have to check now and again that our children understand the ethos of our family unit and why it is different from the one next door and why their friends may be allowed some things that they are not.

Make sure you are on course and your helpers don't misunderstand you. Make sure anyone you invite on your journey understands where you're going. If they are aiming in another direction, it will be wise to part ways than to encounter casualties along the way. Out of the twelve, Peter spoke out and got it right. The rest were not sure but were with Jesus anyway for one reason or the other. Be on the same page with your vision builders.

Reflection

> You know who you are and your purpose. Replicate it in the people who matter so they can carry your spirit and your burden.

Further Reading:

> Mark 8.

Day 29

When You Don't Know What To Say

> *"Peter said to Jesus, 'Rabbi, it is good for us to be here. Let us put up three shelters - one for you, one for Moses and one for Elijah.' (He did not know what to say, they were so frightened.) Then a cloud appeared and covered them, and a voice came from the cloud: 'This is my Son, whom I love. Listen to him!'"*
>
> Mark 9:4-6

Jesus invited three of his disciples to the top of a mountain for some time alone (as was the custom of Jesus, he often spent time alone in prayer). During this time (I suppose during Jesus' time of meditation), Peter, James and John see Jesus transform into a glorious radiant state with Elijah and Moses having a conversation with Him. Mark does not tell us what they were discussing, but Luke tells us that it was about what would happen in Jerusalem and His departure (Luke 9:31) It was clear that the conversation was between just the three of them. The disciples were not invited to be part of the conversation.

In verse 5, Peter gives a suggestion, some advice, quite unsolicited. He offers his help on an event that has happened without his influence and which is also beyond his understanding. He stated, *"Rabbi, it is good for us to be here. Let us put up three shelters—one for you, one for Moses and one for Elijah."* This was the first time Jesus had spent His alone prayer time with any of his disciples. The second one was in the garden of Gethsemane before His death. And here we have Peter suggesting putting up tents for Jesus, Moses and Elijah.

And why did he make this ridiculous suggestion? Because *"He did not know what to say, they were so frightened."*

Sometimes when you don't know what to say, it's best to say nothing. Peter said a bowl of nonsense really because he was afraid and did not know what to say.

It comes down to protocol and knowing your place. We save ourselves a lot of grief when we know when it's not about us. Sometimes we have to step away from a situation and allow the stakeholders to make their decision no matter how emotionally involved we are.

Peter was justified for being frightened, but his emotions led him to say something that was not appropriate to say. Do not let your emotions make you react; you don't have to do something in response to your emotions. Learn to stay calm whenever your emotions get a greater part of you. As a result, he received a rebuke directly from God. This would have worsened his fear - God telling him off right from heaven!

So the next time you don't know what to say, say nothing. When you're emotionally charged, be silent. And don't give advice based on your insecurities.

Reflection

> Ask the Lord to give you self-control over your emotions, especially the negative emotions.

Further Reading:

> 2 Peter 1.

Day 30

Loved, so Corrected

> *"'I am with you and will save you, declares the Lord. 'Though I completely destroy all the nations among which I scatter you, I will not completely destroy you. I will discipline you but only in due measure; I will not let you go entirely unpunished.'"*
>
> Jeremiah 30:11

In the book of Jeremiah, the people of God sinned greatly against the Lord, they were corrupt, worshipped idols and unrepentant. The Lord sent them this warning through His prophet but the message was bittersweet. It was sweet as in *"I am with you and I will save you"* and bitter because the Lord promised to punish them in *"due measure."*

This is a God who loves and disciplines His children. He will punish the other nations who messed about with Judah and then he will punish Judah for going astray and copying the heathen nations. He won't just cover Judah's sins because Judah is His beloved. God punishes his children for the purpose of correction, not destruction. He punishes the unbelievers to destruction so the earth will be purged of sin but not so His children. We are his seed, so He corrects us so we can be clean and shine brighter. When we go astray, He corrects us - *"... God disciplines us for our good, in order that we may share in his holiness."* (Hebrews 12:10)

In our journey to fruitfulness as children of God, we understand that God is our Heavenly Father, who parents exceedingly better than any earthly father. He loves us, cares for us, provides for us, protects us and as part of His love for us, disciplines us.

Again He tells us He'll discipline us in due measure.

> *"'Do not be afraid, Jacob my servant, for I am with you,' declares the Lord. 'Though I completely destroy all the nations among which I scatter you, I will not completely destroy you. I will discipline you but only in due measure; I will not let you go entirely unpunished.'"*
>
> *Jeremiah 46:28*

It would be unjust for God to punish those who don't know Him and pat us on the back just because we are His. He's a just God. Sin has a consequence. If you're a child of God, you have to be like your father God. If we meddle in sin - any kind of sin, the Lord will forgive us and correct us. Whether in the open or behind closed doors, God sees; so if we claim His love and every good thing about Him, then we must accept the responsibility of discipline that comes with the rights of being a child of God. We're corrected because we're loved.

Reflection

> Is there any consequence of sin you're dealing with right now? Repent and ask the Lord for forgiveness. Ask the Lord to lead you back to perfect fellowship with Him.

Further Reading:

> Jeremiah 30.

Day 31

Giving

"Not that I desire your gifts; what I desire is that more be credited to your account."

Philippians 4:17

In my quest for fruitfulness, I have come to the truth that giving to support God's vision plays an important role in fruitfulness.

In the scripture above, the Philippian church had sent some supplies to Paul who was on a missionary journey. Paul was accomplishing a much-needed outreach to Europe and was blessed by the supplies sent by the Philippian church. But he told them that *"what I desire is that more be credited to your account"*. The receipt of the gift was secondary as far as he was concerned. When we give to facilitate God's will, more is credited to our account. Our giving goes as a gift to the receiver but also as a reward of a harvest to us. Unless we give, we deny ourselves this reward of harvest.

Giving to God's vision is a matter of priority before any good deeds. And let's just clarify that such giving is not good deeds, it is a service of love to God. It is an opportune moment that unlocks the blessings of heaven upon us. When the woman with the alabaster box poured her expensive fragrance to anoint Jesus, everyone in the room was disappointed but Jesus interpreted the incident differently.

> *"The poor you will always have with you, and you can help them any time you want. But you will not always have me. She did what she could. She poured perfume on my body beforehand to prepare for My burial. Truly I tell you, wherever the gospel*

> *is preached throughout the world, what she has done will also be told, in memory of her."*
>
> Mark 14:7-9

Giving to the poor is not the same as giving to the Lord. This woman met the Lord's need to prepare His body before His death.

What does the Lord need of you? It could be a monetary giving to your church so the heating bills can be paid for the month. It could be regular visits to that lonely person who needs company. It could be a word of encouragement to the teenager who admires you and wants to be like you. Your godly voice could make a difference in their lives.

Support God's vision with your substance and as you do so, He will bless you and credit it to your account. We'll always have the poor with us. Philanthropists have been giving since time immemorial but the poverty level in the world has not changed. It's good to support charities who give to good causes, but the greatest cause you can give to, is towards God's vision. This is a the catalyst that *"opens the windows of heaven"* (Malachi 3:10).

Reflection

> Prayerfully consider where to sow your seed. Ask the Holy Spirit to guide you to the right need that touches His heart.

Further Reading:

> 2 Corinthians 9.

...

Also in Eva's Daily Devotional Series

Wisdom for Victory

This début book of her series is a 31-day devotional that will guide you in a step-by-step journey to strengthening your relationship with God. You don't have to be a Christian defeated by the world and by life. Lift high your banner of victory as you embark on this journey of discovery into the heart of your Father and your identity as a child of God. Buckle up, it's going to be an exciting journey that's Heaven-bound and earthly-relevant!

ISBN: 978-1-90797-163-1

Available from Eva, her Publisher and on Amazon.

www.ingramcontent.com/pod-product-compliance
Lightning Source LLC
Chambersburg PA
CBHW071751040426
42446CB00012B/2522